The Hist

Embarking on a Historical Expedition

Emergence of a Land: Uruguay's Geological Origins

The story of Uruguay's geological origins traces back millions of years, revealing the intricate processes that shaped this land into what it is today. This chapter delves into the fascinating tale of tectonic shifts, ancient seas, and the slow dance of time that molded Uruguay's diverse landscapes.

Uruguay's journey began during the Precambrian era, over 1.7 billion years ago, when the earth's crust began to form. Vast movements of tectonic plates led to the creation of the Rio de la Plata Craton, a core foundation of Uruguay's geology. Throughout eons, this craton became a resilient base, resisting the forces of erosion and upheaval.

As time marched on, oceans came and went. In the early Paleozoic era, around 500 million years ago, shallow seas covered much of Uruguay's territory. The slow accumulation of sedimentary deposits over millions of years created layers of limestone, sandstone, and shale, preserving a geological history that tells tales of ancient marine life and environmental changes.

Fast forward to the Mesozoic era, approximately 250 million years ago, and the supercontinent Pangaea began to break apart. Uruguay found itself wedged between fragments of Gondwana, facing the South Atlantic Ocean. This era saw the intrusion of igneous rocks like granites and basalts, as well as the formation of the South Atlantic rift basin, which would later influence the landscape.

The Cretaceous period, about 145 million years ago, witnessed further transformations. The rift basin expanded, welcoming the sea, and depositing layers of sediments rich in gypsum and limestone. Fossilized remains of ancient creatures, like ammonites and marine reptiles, offer glimpses into this distant past.

During the Cenozoic era, about 65 million years ago, the Andes mountain-building process began to shape Uruguay's destiny. The uplift of the Andes sent sediment-filled rivers flowing into the region, depositing layers of sand and clay that would later become essential components of Uruguay's soils. As the climate shifted from tropical to temperate, grasslands emerged, setting the stage for the nation's pastoral future.

Glacial activity, primarily during the Pleistocene epoch around 2.6 million years ago, added a frosty touch to Uruguay's geological tapestry. The advancing and retreating glaciers sculpted the landscape, altering river courses, and contributing to the formation of fertile valleys.

The Holocene epoch, which began around 11,700 years ago, witnessed the dawn of human civilization in Uruguay. Indigenous peoples navigated the diverse landscapes that had evolved over eons, adapting to the changing environments and shaping their societies.

Indigenous Tapestry: Pre-Colonial Cultures of Uruguay

Long before the arrival of European explorers, the land that would later become Uruguay was already inhabited by indigenous peoples whose rich cultures and histories shaped the region. In this chapter, we delve into the intricate tapestry of pre-colonial societies that flourished in what is now Uruguay.

The earliest evidence of human presence in Uruguay dates back to approximately 11,000 years ago, as indicated by archaeological findings. The indigenous populations of this era were likely hunter-gatherers, relying on the resources provided by the diverse landscapes - from coastal areas teeming with marine life to the fertile grasslands rich in game.

As time progressed, different cultural groups emerged, each adapting to their specific environments. Among these were the Charrúa people, known for their nomadic lifestyle and deep connection to the land. They roamed the grasslands, hunting guanacos and rheas, and gathering edible plants. The Charrúas left their mark on the region, influencing its history and even its name, as "Uruguay" is thought to have originated from the Guarani word "urugua" which means "river of painted birds."

Another significant group was the Guaraní, who migrated to Uruguay from the north and brought with them advanced agricultural practices. They cultivated maize, beans, and squash, transforming parts of the landscape into thriving gardens. The Guaraní also had a sophisticated social structure and religious beliefs that influenced the fabric of pre-colonial societies.

Trade networks developed between different indigenous groups, connecting the coastal communities with those living in the interior. These interactions facilitated the exchange of goods such as shells, feathers, and precious stones, fostering cultural exchange and connections across vast distances.

Artistic expression flourished among these societies, leaving behind a legacy of intricate pottery, carvings, and rock art. These artifacts offer glimpses into their beliefs, daily lives, and connections to the spiritual world. Symbolism was woven into their creations, reflecting their reverence for nature and the spiritual realms.

Social organization varied among indigenous groups. Some lived in small, mobile bands, while others established more settled villages. Leadership structures were diverse, ranging from tribal chiefs to spiritual leaders, reflecting the multifaceted nature of their societies.

The arrival of European explorers in the 16th century marked a pivotal turning point for these indigenous cultures. Encounters with the newcomers, often marred by conflict and disease, led to significant disruptions in their ways of life. European diseases, to which the indigenous populations had no immunity, decimated their numbers, leaving many communities devastated.

First Contact: European Exploration and Early Encounters

The dawn of the 16th century marked a significant turning point in Uruguay's history as European explorers embarked on journeys that would forever alter the course of the region's indigenous cultures and landscapes. In this chapter, we delve into the intricate tapestry of the first contact between the indigenous peoples of Uruguay and the explorers from the Old World.

European interest in the Americas was driven by the desire for riches, new trade routes, and the spread of Christianity. Spanish explorers, among the first to set foot on Uruguayan soil, sought to expand their empire and find the rumored wealth of this newly discovered land.

Juan Díaz de Solís, a Spanish explorer, is often credited with being the first European to venture into the Rio de la Plata region, including parts of modern-day Uruguay, in 1516. However, his expedition ended tragically as he and some of his crew were killed during a hostile encounter with indigenous people.

It was the voyage of Ferdinand Magellan's expedition in 1520 that revealed the strategic importance of the Rio de la Plata as a navigational route. This opened the door to further exploration by Spanish conquistadors, including Sebastian Cabot, who explored the region in the early 1520s.

In 1527, Sebastian Cabot's expedition established Fort Sancti Spiritu on the Paraná River, near modern-day Uruguay. The fort was intended to secure Spanish presence and control in the area. However, it faced challenges from indigenous resistance and harsh living conditions, leading to its abandonment.

Subsequent expeditions continued to explore the region's coastlines and rivers, encountering indigenous peoples along the way. These early encounters were marked by a mixture of curiosity, misunderstanding, and conflict. The indigenous populations, unaccustomed to the Europeans and their technologies, often responded with a blend of hospitality and caution.

Explorers like Juan Ortiz de Zárate and Pedro de Mendoza aimed to establish settlements, but their efforts were met with challenges, including harsh weather, inadequate supplies, and resistance from both indigenous peoples and rival European powers.

During these early interactions, the indigenous populations were introduced to European goods such as metal tools, textiles, and firearms. The exchange of goods had far-reaching impacts on their societies and cultures, transforming traditional modes of production and altering social dynamics.

As explorations continued, European diseases took a toll on the indigenous populations, leading to devastating epidemics that drastically reduced their numbers. The introduction of European diseases, to which the indigenous populations had no immunity, decimated their ranks and changed the landscape of Uruguay forever.

The initial contacts also paved the way for further European incursions, leading to the establishment of permanent settlements and the beginning of colonization. The intricate web of encounters, struggles, and cultural exchanges during this period set the stage for the complex history that would unfold in Uruguay in the centuries to come.

Colonial Crucible: Uruguay Under Spanish Rule

The arrival of Spanish conquerors in the early 16th century marked the beginning of a new era for Uruguay, as the region became part of the vast Spanish colonial empire. This chapter delves into the multifaceted dynamics of Uruguay's colonial history, exploring the intricate tapestry woven through centuries of Spanish rule.

The Spanish Crown's interest in the new world was driven by a combination of economic ambitions, religious zeal, and the desire to expand its influence. Spain sought to extract wealth from its colonies while simultaneously spreading Christianity and establishing control over distant lands.

The establishment of the Viceroyalty of Peru in 1542 extended Spanish authority over Uruguay, as the region fell within its jurisdiction. The indigenous populations of Uruguay were gradually subjected to Spanish domination, with encomiendas and later repartimientos becoming systems of forced labor, causing significant upheaval in indigenous societies.

The early settlements of Montevideo and Colonia del Sacramento, founded respectively by the Spanish in 1726 and the Portuguese in 1680, became focal points of colonial activity. Montevideo developed as a strategic port, facilitating trade and communication between the Spanish colonies and Europe, while Colonia del Sacramento's location led to conflicts between Spanish and Portuguese interests. The Spanish crown established a system of governance that divided the region into encomiendas and later corregimientos. Spanish settlers, often referred to as "peninsulares," held positions of power and authority, while the indigenous populations and African slaves were subjected to labor and exploitation.

The introduction of European crops and livestock transformed the landscape of Uruguay, as the Spanish introduced wheat, maize, cattle, and horses. These changes had profound impacts on the environment, indigenous cultures, and the economy, as traditional modes of subsistence shifted.

Religion played a central role in colonial life, as the Spanish sought to convert the indigenous populations to Christianity. Missions and churches were established, often in proximity to indigenous settlements, shaping the cultural and spiritual landscape of Uruguay. Throughout the colonial period, Uruguay experienced geopolitical conflicts, as European powers vied for control over the region. The Treaty of Madrid in 1750 settled disputes between Spain and Portugal, resulting in Colonia del Sacramento being ceded to the Spanish. However, tensions persisted, reflecting the broader global struggles of colonial powers.

The late 18th century brought significant changes to Uruguay's colonial landscape. Enlightenment ideas and increasing discontent with Spanish rule led to movements for independence across the Americas. Uruguay was not exempt from these influences, as criollos (those of Spanish descent born in the Americas) began to question their position within the colonial hierarchy.

Struggles for Independence: Uruguay's Fight for Autonomy

The 19th century brought forth a wave of fervor for independence across Latin America, and Uruguay was no exception. This chapter delves into the intricate tapestry of Uruguay's fight for autonomy, as the region embarked on a tumultuous journey toward liberation from Spanish colonial rule.

As the ideas of enlightenment and revolution spread throughout the Americas, the people of Uruguay began to question their allegiance to the Spanish crown. Influenced by the successes of other independence movements, including those of neighboring countries like Argentina and Brazil, Uruguayans yearned for self-determination and the chance to shape their destiny.

Uruguay's path to independence was shaped by a series of conflicts, alliances, and shifting loyalties. The region was caught in the crossfire of broader geopolitical struggles between European powers, as well as regional rivalries. The Spanish crown's weakening grip on its colonies further fueled aspirations for autonomy.

The early 19th century saw the rise of local leaders and revolutionary movements. Leaders like José Gervasio Artigas emerged as symbols of resistance against Spanish rule. Artigas, known for his charismatic leadership and advocacy for the rights of common people, rallied support for the cause of independence.

The Battle of Las Piedras in 1811 marked a pivotal moment in Uruguay's struggle for autonomy. Under the leadership of Artigas, Uruguayan forces achieved a decisive victory against Spanish royalist forces. This success boosted the morale of independence advocates and strengthened the resolve to break free from colonial control.

However, Uruguay's path to independence was far from linear. Internal divisions, power struggles, and external pressures complicated the process. The region's location between powerful neighbors like Argentina and Brazil made it a strategic battleground for competing interests.

In 1816, the region declared its independence as the "Provincia Oriental del Río de la Plata." Yet, this declaration did not lead to immediate self-governance. The Congress of Tucumán, which aimed to establish a united South American republic, cast uncertainty over Uruguay's status, leading to conflicts between regional leaders and central authorities.

The struggle for autonomy also witnessed foreign intervention. Brazil, under the rule of the Portuguese crown, sought to assert control over Uruguay, leading to a series of conflicts known as the Cisplatine War. Uruguayans faced the challenge of repelling both Spanish and Brazilian forces, further testing their resolve for self-determination.

The constant upheavals eventually led to the establishment of the "Provisional Triple Alliance," a coalition of Uruguay, Argentina, and Brazil united against foreign intervention. The alliance's victory in the Battle of Caseros in 1852 dealt a blow to Brazilian interests in Uruguay, paving the way for a new phase of the region's struggle for autonomy.

Uruguay's path to full independence was solidified in 1828 with the signing of the Treaty of Montevideo, which recognized Uruguay as a sovereign state. The nation's first constitution was adopted in 1830, solidifying its status as an independent entity.

The struggles for independence left an indelible mark on Uruguay's national identity. The tumultuous journey highlighted the resilience, determination, and unity of the people in their pursuit of autonomy. As we explore this chapter, we unravel the complexities and sacrifices that shaped Uruguay's emergence as an independent nation.

Birth of a Nation: The Formation of Uruguay in the 19th Century

The 19th century marked a transformative period in Uruguay's history, as the region emerged from the struggles for independence to solidify its identity as a sovereign nation. This chapter delves into the intricate tapestry of Uruguay's formation as a nation-state, exploring the political, social, and cultural developments that shaped its trajectory.

The early years of the 19th century were marked by political instability and power struggles as Uruguay sought to define its identity and establish a stable government. The country's first constitution was adopted in 1830, laying the groundwork for the nation's political framework. This constitution set the tone for representative democracy, dividing power among three branches of government.

Uruguay's formation was not without challenges. The country was caught in the midst of regional rivalries and external pressures. The conflicts with neighboring powers, such as Argentina and Brazil, continued to shape Uruguay's destiny as it navigated alliances and disputes.

The political landscape in Uruguay was characterized by a series of internal conflicts and revolutions. The rise of caudillos, charismatic military leaders, played a significant role in shaping the nation's politics. These caudillos often aligned with different factions, leading to periods of instability and armed clashes. The development of political parties also became a defining feature of Uruguay's nation-building process. The Colorados and Blancos emerged as the two main parties, representing different social and ideological groups. Their rivalry and competition for power would continue to influence the country's political landscape for decades to come.

One of the defining moments in Uruguay's formation was the Great Siege of Montevideo (1843-1851), a conflict between the Colorados and Blancos that highlighted the nation's deep divisions. The siege brought international involvement, with foreign powers providing support to different factions. This conflict ultimately culminated in a period of civil war, marked by violence and social upheaval.

The end of the civil war brought a gradual process of reconciliation and stabilization. The political leaders recognized the need for a new constitution that would address the nation's challenges and unite its fragmented society. The Constitution of 1866 established a more balanced and inclusive political framework, setting the stage for a more cohesive nation.

The late 19th century saw significant economic and social transformations in Uruguay. The nation's economy evolved from its agrarian roots to include industry and trade. Infrastructure development, such as railways and telegraph lines, contributed to increased connectivity and growth.

Education and culture also played vital roles in Uruguay's nation-building. The country invested in public education, fostering a literate and informed citizenry. Cultural institutions, including theaters, literary circles, and newspapers, contributed to a vibrant intellectual scene that shaped the nation's cultural identity.

The Art of Progress: Cultural Developments in the 1800s

The 19th century was a period of significant cultural evolution in Uruguay, as the nation sought to define its identity and shape its artistic and intellectual landscape. This chapter delves into the intricate tapestry of cultural developments that unfolded during this transformative era.

The early 1800s marked the beginnings of a vibrant literary scene in Uruguay. As the nation sought to establish its identity, writers and poets emerged as crucial figures in shaping the cultural narrative. Literary societies and circles provided platforms for intellectual exchange and the exploration of national themes.

One of the key literary figures of the era was Juan Zorrilla de San Martín, whose works such as "Tabaré" celebrated Uruguay's indigenous heritage and portrayed the nation's landscape with vivid imagery. This literary masterpiece helped solidify the connection between literature and national identity.

The establishment of the National Library of Uruguay in 1816 underscored the nation's commitment to education and cultural preservation. This institution became a repository of knowledge and a symbol of Uruguay's dedication to intellectual growth.

The 1800s also witnessed the emergence of a flourishing theater scene. The Teatro Solís, founded in 1856 in Montevideo, became a cultural hub hosting both local and international performances. The theater not only entertained audiences but also fostered artistic innovation and cultural exchange.

Visual arts experienced growth as well. The formation of the National Academy of Fine Arts in 1843 provided a formal education in the arts and promoted the development of local talent. Painters like Juan Manuel Blanes gained recognition for their depictions of historical and cultural scenes.

Music played a pivotal role in Uruguay's cultural landscape during the 1800s. The nation's rich musical heritage was influenced by European traditions and local rhythms. Composer Leandro Gómez earned acclaim for his works that celebrated Uruguay's national identity through music.

The cultural developments of this era were intertwined with political and social changes. The struggles for independence and the formation of the nation influenced artistic expression, as creators sought to capture the essence of Uruguay's identity and aspirations.

The intellectual sphere flourished as well, with the emergence of philosophical debates and discussions. Thinkers like José Enrique Rodó explored concepts of national identity, cultural progress, and the role of the individual in society. These ideas contributed to the shaping of Uruguay's intellectual landscape.

The spread of education further fueled cultural growth. Public schools were established to promote literacy and knowledge among the population. The rise of newspapers and literary magazines facilitated the exchange of ideas and intellectual discourse.

Turbulent Times: Political Instability and Conflicts

The 19th century was a period of political turbulence in Uruguay, as the young nation navigated a landscape marked by power struggles, ideological divides, and external pressures. This chapter delves into the intricate tapestry of political instability and conflicts that shaped Uruguay's trajectory during this tumultuous era.

The nation's early years were characterized by a series of internal conflicts that underscored the challenges of forging a unified identity. The rivalry between the Colorados and Blancos political factions intensified, leading to periods of civil unrest and armed clashes. These conflicts often revolved around issues of power, representation, and regional interests.

The Colorados and Blancos emerged as the two main political parties, representing distinct social and ideological groups. This political polarization not only permeated governance but also extended into broader society, fostering divisions that would persist for generations.

The foreign intervention further complicated Uruguay's political landscape. The Cisplatine War (1825-1828) against Brazil highlighted the nation's vulnerability to external pressures. The war culminated in Uruguay's declaration of independence, but it also revealed the challenges of maintaining sovereignty amid regional rivalries.

The international community's recognition of Uruguay's independence was tied to the Treaty of Montevideo in 1828. This marked a significant step in securing the nation's autonomy, but it did not bring an end to internal conflicts. Uruguay continued to grapple with power struggles, rebellions, and territorial disputes.

The mid-19th century witnessed the rise of caudillos, charismatic military leaders who often sought to fill the power vacuum left by political instability. These caudillos established personal fiefdoms and wielded authority over their respective territories. Their leadership contributed to both stability and fragmentation, further shaping the nation's trajectory.

The Great Siege of Montevideo (1843-1851) stands as a prominent example of Uruguay's internal conflicts. This civil war pitted the Colorados against the Blancos, with foreign powers backing different factions. The siege brought violence and destruction, leaving a lasting impact on the nation's collective memory.

External forces continued to influence Uruguay's fate. The Uruguayan War (1864-1865), also known as the War of the Triple Alliance, saw Uruguay allied with Argentina and Brazil against Paraguay. The conflict resulted in further devastation and loss of life, highlighting the complex interplay of regional interests.

The political landscape began to shift in the latter half of the 19th century. The Constitution of 1866 established a more balanced political framework, promoting a sense of stability. This period saw efforts to reconcile differences and move towards a more cohesive nation.

Shaping Identity: Language, Literature, and Nationalism

The quest for identity in Uruguay was intricately woven through its language, literature, and the burgeoning spirit of nationalism. The 19th century saw a nation in flux, seeking to define itself amidst political upheavals and cultural influences. This chapter delves into the multifaceted interactions between language, literature, and nationalism that played a pivotal role in shaping Uruguay's sense of self.

Language stood at the heart of Uruguay's identity formation. Spanish became the linguistic cornerstone, as the nation embraced its colonial legacy while adapting the language to reflect its own evolving character. The Spanish spoken in Uruguay bore traces of regional nuances, influenced by indigenous languages, African dialects, and European immigration.

Literature emerged as a powerful tool for cultural expression and identity formation. Writers and poets became the storytellers of Uruguay's journey, capturing the nation's spirit, values, and aspirations. Works like Juan Zorrilla de San Martín's "Tabaré" celebrated indigenous heritage, intertwining history and myth to weave a narrative of national pride.

The emergence of literary societies and journals provided platforms for intellectual discourse. Literary circles fostered discussions about national identity, politics, and societal progress. These forums became spaces where writers grappled with questions of what it meant to be Uruguayan.

The intersection of literature and nationalism gave rise to a sense of shared cultural identity. Authors sought to highlight the distinct features of Uruguayan culture while also challenging prevailing norms. This effort contributed to the nation's growing awareness of its unique place in the world.

Uruguay's literary figures played a significant role in nurturing a sense of national belonging. José Enrique Rodó's essay "Ariel" explored the tension between European and American values, encouraging Uruguayans to embrace their own cultural identity. This work resonated not only within the nation but also across Latin America.

The celebration of cultural heritage extended to the visual arts as well. Painters and artists sought to capture the nation's landscapes, history, and people. These artistic representations further solidified the connection between creativity and national identity.

The sense of nationalism also found expression in political movements. Leaders like José Gervasio Artigas and his call for federalism echoed a desire for self-governance and unity. Artigas's influence reached beyond politics, as his legacy became intertwined with Uruguay's identity.

Education played a significant role in nurturing a shared identity. The establishment of public schools facilitated widespread literacy and provided a platform for imparting national values and history. As Uruguayan children learned about their country's past, they also became part of its future.

The role of literature and language in shaping identity was exemplified by the formation of institutions like the Uruguayan Academy of Language. This organization aimed to safeguard the purity of the Spanish language and promote linguistic unity, emphasizing the importance of language in forging a cohesive national identity.

Gauchos and Estancias: Uruguay's Rural Heritage

Uruguay's rural heritage is deeply intertwined with its iconic gauchos and sprawling estancias, embodying the nation's historical connection to the land and its pastoral traditions. This chapter delves into the multifaceted tapestry of Uruguay's rural life, exploring the roles of gauchos, the significance of estancias, and the lasting impact on the nation's identity.

The gaucho, a legendary figure in Uruguayan history, represents the spirit of the nation's rural population. These skilled horsemen and ranch workers inhabited the vast grasslands, or pampas, where they navigated the challenges of herding livestock, surviving in the wilderness, and mastering traditional horsemanship.

The origins of the gaucho can be traced back to the colonial period, as Spanish colonizers introduced cattle and horses to the region. Over time, the gaucho emerged as a distinct social group, characterized by their unique dress, lifestyle, and cultural practices. Their contribution to Uruguay's identity was profound, influencing art, literature, and national folklore.

The estancia, vast ranches that dot the countryside, became the cornerstone of Uruguay's rural landscape. These sprawling estates were centers of agricultural and livestock production, serving as hubs of economic activity and cultural exchange. Estancias played a pivotal role in shaping Uruguay's economy and social fabric.

Livestock farming, particularly cattle ranching, became a cornerstone of Uruguay's economy. The fertile grasslands of the pampas provided an ideal environment for cattle to thrive, leading to the growth of the beef industry. Estancias focused on raising cattle for meat and leather, establishing Uruguay as a significant player in the global market.

The estancias' vast landscapes also had a profound impact on Uruguayan culture and identity. They served as settings for traditional rural activities, such as rodeos and folk festivals. The estancia lifestyle fostered a sense of community among those who lived and worked on the ranches, shaping a shared identity based on rural values.

The gaucho's influence extended beyond the estancias, reaching into art, literature, and music. Gaucho-inspired folk music, such as milonga and candombe, became an integral part of Uruguay's cultural heritage. Writers and poets celebrated the gaucho's way of life, immortalizing their tales of bravery, camaraderie, and resilience.

The estancia lifestyle and gaucho culture were not without challenges. Economic fluctuations, technological advancements, and shifts in global demand impacted the rural way of life. Modernization and urbanization brought changes to the landscape, altering the balance between rural and urban spheres.

In the late 19th and early 20th centuries, the gaucho figure experienced a revival through literary works, music, and cultural events. This resurgence reflected a desire to preserve and honor Uruguay's rural heritage in the face of evolving times.

Today, Uruguay's rural heritage remains an essential part of the nation's identity. Estancias continue to operate as centers of agricultural production, offering visitors a glimpse into the past while embracing modern sustainability practices. The legacy of the gaucho endures through cultural celebrations, art, and a collective pride in the nation's rural roots.

Railways and Urbanization: Transformation of Urban Spaces

The late 19th and early 20th centuries witnessed a transformative period in Uruguay's history, marked by the introduction of railways and the consequent urbanization that reshaped the nation's urban spaces. This chapter delves into the multifaceted tapestry of this era, exploring the roles of railways, the impact on urban development, and the lasting legacy on Uruguay's urban landscape.

The advent of railways in Uruguay marked a significant technological advancement. Railways not only revolutionized transportation but also catalyzed economic growth and social change. The first railway line, connecting the capital city of Montevideo to the town of Bella Vista, was inaugurated in 1869, heralding a new era of connectivity.

The expansion of railways transformed the movement of goods and people, connecting urban centers to rural areas and fostering economic integration. Railways facilitated the transport of agricultural products, including beef and wool, from the interior to the coast for export. This laid the foundation for Uruguay's role as a key player in global trade.

Urbanization was a natural consequence of railway development. The increased ease of travel brought about by railways prompted population movement from rural areas to urban centers. Cities like Montevideo experienced rapid growth as people sought opportunities for work, education, and improved living standards.

The railway network also enabled the emergence of commuter towns and suburbs. Workers could now live farther from the city center and commute daily, leading to the expansion of urban areas beyond traditional boundaries. This urban sprawl marked the beginning of a new phase in Uruguay's urban development.

The introduction of railways influenced urban planning and architecture. Stations became focal points of activity, leading to the establishment of new neighborhoods around them. The architecture of railway stations often combined functional design with grandeur, reflecting the importance of railways in the nation's progress.

The transformation of urban spaces was not limited to infrastructure. The growth of cities brought about changes in social dynamics, cultural activities, and the emergence of new urban lifestyles. The influx of diverse populations contributed to the enrichment of urban culture and the development of a cosmopolitan identity.

Urban amenities and services expanded in response to the growing population. The establishment of schools, hospitals, and cultural institutions catered to the needs of the urban populace. This period of urbanization laid the groundwork for modern urban infrastructure and services.

The influence of railways on urbanization reached beyond Montevideo. Cities like Salto, Paysandú, and Tacuarembó experienced growth as railway lines extended their reach. These cities became hubs of economic activity, trade, and cultural exchange, contributing to a more interconnected nation.

As the 20th century progressed, automobiles and other forms of transportation began to challenge the dominance of railways. The decline of railways as the primary mode of transportation led to shifts in urban development patterns, and some railway lines were eventually decommissioned.

However, the legacy of railways and urbanization remains embedded in Uruguay's urban fabric. The railway stations that once served as points of departure and arrival continue to hold cultural and historical significance. The transformed urban spaces bear witness to a period of growth, change, and evolution that shaped the nation's identity.

The era of railways and urbanization stands as a testament to Uruguay's commitment to progress and modernization. As we explore this chapter, we uncover the layers of transformation, connectivity, and urban growth that have left an indelible mark on Uruguay's urban landscape.

Footsteps of Modernity: Technological Advances and Industrialization

The 20th century ushered in a period of unprecedented change for Uruguay, characterized by technological advances and the embrace of industrialization. This chapter delves into the multifaceted tapestry of this era, exploring the roles of technological innovations, the impact on industry, and the lasting legacy on Uruguay's path to modernity.

The early 20th century witnessed the integration of technological innovations that transformed various aspects of Uruguayan society. The expansion of electricity and telecommunication networks brought newfound connectivity, revolutionizing communication, commerce, and daily life.

The automotive industry emerged as a driving force of change. The introduction of automobiles revolutionized transportation, transforming the way people moved within and between urban and rural areas. Automobiles became symbols of status and freedom, shaping the nation's cultural landscape.

Industrialization gained momentum as Uruguay sought to diversify its economy and decrease reliance on traditional agricultural exports. The growth of manufacturing industries led to increased production of textiles, food products, and machinery. Factories became hubs of employment and contributed to economic growth.

The introduction of modern agricultural techniques and machinery revolutionized farming practices. Mechanization increased productivity, leading to greater efficiency in the production of crops and livestock. This shift marked a departure from traditional agricultural methods and positioned Uruguay as a modern agricultural player.

Urbanization continued to accelerate alongside industrialization. The expansion of factories and increased job opportunities in urban centers attracted people from rural areas. Cities like Montevideo experienced further growth, leading to changes in urban landscapes, housing, and infrastructure.

The growth of industry also led to changes in labor dynamics. Labor unions emerged as workers sought better working conditions, fair wages, and improved rights. Strikes and protests became vehicles for expressing labor demands and influencing national policy.

The technological advancements and industrialization of this era were closely tied to education and research. The establishment of technical schools and universities equipped the nation with skilled professionals who contributed to technological development and innovation.

Urban planning and architecture responded to the demands of industrialization. New urban spaces, factories, and residential areas were designed to accommodate the changing needs of a modernizing society. Urban development projects aimed to balance economic progress with quality of life.

The era also saw efforts to diversify energy sources. Hydropower plants were established, harnessing the nation's water resources to generate electricity. This move toward renewable energy reflected Uruguay's commitment to sustainability and technological progress.

The impact of technological advances and industrialization extended to cultural spheres as well. Art, literature, and music responded to the changing times, reflecting themes of progress, urban life, and the challenges of modernity.

Cultural Renaissance: Fine Arts and Intellectual Flourishing

The latter half of the 20th century brought forth a cultural renaissance in Uruguay, characterized by a flourishing of fine arts and a vibrant intellectual scene. This chapter delves into the intricate tapestry of this era, exploring the roles of artists, intellectuals, and the lasting impact on Uruguay's cultural landscape.

The post-war period saw a reinvigoration of the fine arts in Uruguay. Artists sought to break away from conventional norms and embrace innovative forms of expression. Painting, sculpture, and visual arts flourished as creators experimented with new techniques and styles.

The emergence of the Torres García Workshop in the 1940s played a pivotal role in shaping Uruguay's artistic identity. Joaquín Torres García, an influential artist and thinker, established the workshop as a hub of artistic exploration and intellectual dialogue. The workshop's teachings emphasized abstraction, symbolism, and a renewed appreciation for indigenous and pre-Columbian art.

Uruguayan artists gained recognition both nationally and internationally. Painters like Pedro Figari captured the nation's essence through his vibrant, evocative landscapes and scenes of everyday life. His work reflected Uruguay's cultural diversity and its deep connection to its people and surroundings. Literature also experienced a renaissance, with writers and poets contributing to a rich literary landscape. The influence of modernism and existentialism led to introspective and experimental works that explored the human experience, identity, and societal dynamics.

Intellectual circles flourished during this era, fostering dialogue and debates on philosophical, social, and political matters. Thinkers like Carlos Vaz Ferreira and Emir Rodríguez Monegal became influential figures in shaping intellectual discourse and advancing cultural thought.

The 1960s witnessed a surge in political and social activism, with artists and intellectuals playing a significant role. Cultural expressions such as theater, music, and visual arts became platforms for dissent and reflection. The era saw a fusion of art and politics, leading to a new wave of creative and thought-provoking works.

Cinema also gained prominence as a means of cultural expression. Filmmakers like Juan Carlos Onetti and Mario Handler brought Uruguayan stories to the screen, reflecting societal realities and exploring themes of identity and belonging.

The return to democracy in the 1980s further nurtured cultural growth. Freedom of expression and creativity flourished as artists and intellectuals contributed to a dynamic cultural landscape. New forms of media, including television and radio, became outlets for cultural dissemination and dialogue.

Uruguay's cultural renaissance left a lasting impact on the nation's identity. The creativity, innovation, and intellectual vibrancy of this era continue to shape the arts, literature, and societal conversations in contemporary Uruguay.

Forging Democracy: Political Evolution in the Early 20th Century

The early 20th century marked a period of political evolution in Uruguay, as the nation navigated a path towards democracy amidst shifting ideologies, social changes, and regional dynamics. This chapter delves into the multifaceted tapestry of this era, exploring the roles of political parties, constitutional reforms, and the lasting impact on Uruguay's democratic foundations.

The dawn of the 20th century saw Uruguay as a nation undergoing significant transformations. A growing middle class, urbanization, and technological advancements set the stage for a changing political landscape. The nation sought to reconcile its diverse social fabric and craft a political system that would reflect the aspirations of its people.

Political parties played a central role in shaping Uruguay's political evolution. The Colorados and Blancos continued to be dominant players, but the political scene also witnessed the emergence of new parties that represented various ideological currents. This pluralism laid the foundation for democratic competition and discourse.

The Batllismo era, marked by the presidency of José Batlle y Ordóñez, stands as a pivotal period in Uruguay's political development. Batlle y Ordóñez introduced a series of reforms that sought to promote social justice, education, and workers' rights. His legacy left an indelible mark on the nation's political philosophy and social policies.

Constitutional reforms played a crucial role in shaping Uruguay's democratic foundations. The Constitution of 1917 established key principles such as the separation of church and state, universal suffrage, and the establishment of an independent judiciary. These reforms aimed to ensure a more inclusive and representative political system.

The influence of the working class and labor movements also grew during this era. The establishment of labor unions and the emergence of leftist parties reflected the changing social dynamics. The demands for workers' rights and social welfare contributed to the evolution of Uruguay's political agenda.

Women's suffrage was another significant milestone in Uruguay's political evolution. The nation became a pioneer in granting women the right to vote in 1927, positioning itself as a progressive leader in gender equality. This move highlighted Uruguay's commitment to inclusivity and representation.

The early 20th century also witnessed shifts in regional dynamics. The rise of authoritarian regimes in neighboring countries, such as Argentina and Brazil, underscored Uruguay's commitment to democratic principles. The nation's determination to preserve its democratic identity became even more pronounced in the face of regional challenges.

The interplay between political parties and a dynamic civil society further nurtured Uruguay's democratic growth. Civic engagement, intellectual discussions, and a vibrant press contributed to a climate of political accountability and public discourse.

The democratic foundations laid during this era continue to shape Uruguay's political landscape. The nation's commitment to democratic values, inclusivity, and social justice remains integral to its identity. The early 20th century stands as a testament to Uruguay's journey towards forging a political system that reflects the aspirations and rights of its people.

Global Ripples: Uruguay's Role in World Wars and International Relations

The 20th century brought Uruguay onto the global stage, as the nation grappled with the impacts of two World Wars and navigated a complex web of international relations. This chapter delves into the intricate tapestry of Uruguay's involvement in world conflicts, its diplomatic endeavors, and the lasting impact on its global position.

World War I, which erupted in 1914, had far-reaching effects that extended beyond Europe. Uruguay, although geographically distant from the theater of war, felt the repercussions of the conflict. The nation's economy was closely tied to international trade, and disruptions caused by the war influenced trade patterns and economic stability.

Uruguay managed to remain neutral during World War I, a stance that reflected its commitment to peace and non-intervention in international conflicts. This neutrality, however, did not shield the nation from the economic challenges brought about by disrupted trade routes and fluctuating markets.

The aftermath of World War I led to a reevaluation of global power dynamics. The League of Nations, established as a forum for international cooperation and conflict resolution, captured Uruguay's attention. The nation joined the League of Nations, contributing to diplomatic discussions and participating in efforts to maintain global peace and stability.

The interwar period marked a time of shifting alliances and emerging international challenges. Uruguay's focus on diplomacy and its commitment to neutrality positioned the nation as a mediator in regional conflicts. The nation's dedication to peace resonated with its global counterparts and contributed to its growing international reputation.

World War II brought new challenges to Uruguay's doorstep. The nation, once again committed to maintaining its neutrality, found itself grappling with the complexities of a world engulfed in war. The impact of the war on international trade, as well as the migration of refugees fleeing the conflict, reached Uruguayan shores.

Despite its neutral stance, Uruguay's position was not without controversy. The nation's decision to maintain diplomatic relations with Axis powers, particularly Germany, raised eyebrows and led to debates over the nation's role in global affairs. The challenges of balancing neutrality with international expectations highlighted the complexities of navigating a world at war.

After World War II, Uruguay continued to engage in diplomatic efforts aimed at fostering international cooperation. The nation supported the establishment of the United Nations and actively participated in discussions on global issues. Uruguay's commitment to peace and multilateralism underscored its role as a responsible global citizen.

The nation's international engagements extended beyond diplomacy. Uruguay's participation in international sports events, such as the Olympics and the World Cup, showcased its prowess on the global stage and fostered a sense of national pride.

Uruguay's role in World Wars and international relations left a lasting impact on its global position and diplomatic legacy. The nation's commitment to neutrality, peace, and cooperation resonates with its contemporary approach to international affairs. The tumultuous 20th century stands as a testament to Uruguay's resilience, diplomatic acumen, and its place in the world arena.

Sporting Passion: Soccer's Deep Roots in Uruguayan Society

Soccer, or football as it is commonly known in Uruguay, holds a special place in the hearts of its people. The history of soccer in the country is deeply intertwined with its culture, identity, and sense of national pride. This chapter delves into the intricate tapestry of soccer's journey in Uruguay, exploring its origins, the role of clubs, international success, and its lasting impact on society.

Soccer found its way to Uruguay in the late 19th century, introduced by British expatriates and sailors who brought the game to the port cities. The simplicity of the sport, its accessibility, and the sense of camaraderie it fostered quickly captured the imagination of Uruguayan youth.

Local clubs played a pivotal role in shaping the sport's trajectory. The establishment of the first soccer club, Central Uruguay Railway Cricket Club (CURCC), in 1891 marked the official entry of soccer into Uruguayan society. Other clubs soon followed suit, and these institutions became not only centers of athletic competition but also social and cultural hubs.

The rivalry between clubs, particularly CURCC and Albion, contributed to the popularization of the sport. Matches between these early clubs drew enthusiastic crowds and laid the groundwork for the fervent soccer culture that would later engulf the nation.

Uruguay's passion for soccer culminated in a historic moment: the triumph in the 1924 Paris Olympics. The Uruguayan national team, known as La Celeste, won the gold medal, marking a turning point for Uruguayan soccer on the international stage. This victory ignited a sense of national pride and solidified soccer's position as a unifying force.

The 1930 FIFA World Cup held in Uruguay stands as a defining moment in soccer history. The tournament not only marked the birth of the World Cup but also showcased Uruguay's prowess as the host nation. Uruguay's victory in the tournament's final against Argentina, in front of a passionate home crowd, solidified its reputation as a soccer powerhouse.

The sport's influence extended beyond the pitch. Soccer became ingrained in the fabric of daily life, impacting cultural norms, music, and even politics. The sport's popularity transcended social classes, uniting people from different walks of life in their shared love for the game.

Soccer also became a platform for social change and activism. The "Maracanazo" victory in the 1950 World Cup final against Brazil, held in Brazil's Maracanã Stadium, became a symbol of overcoming adversity and defying the odds. This victory was particularly meaningful given the historical context and the challenges Uruguay faced.

The influence of soccer in Uruguayan society continued to evolve. Clubs like Nacional and Peñarol emerged as fierce rivals, reflecting broader regional and cultural divides. These rivalries heightened the sense of passion and identity tied to the sport.

Soccer's impact reached beyond national borders. Uruguay's contributions to the sport's development, its successes in international competitions, and its passionate fan base earned it a respected place in the global soccer community.

The sport's enduring legacy is reflected in the modern era. Soccer remains a dominant cultural force, with generations of Uruguayans continuing to embrace the sport as an integral part of their lives. The passion for soccer exemplifies the nation's unity, identity, and the powerful role of sports in shaping societal dynamics.

Echoes of Change: Social and Economic Shifts in the Mid-20th Century

The mid-20th century brought about a period of profound change in Uruguay, as the nation navigated social and economic shifts that would shape its trajectory for years to come. This chapter delves into the intricate tapestry of this era, exploring the roles of industrialization, urbanization, social policies, and the lasting impact on Uruguay's society and economy.

The post-World War II period saw Uruguay undergo rapid industrialization. The nation's push for diversification and modernization led to the growth of manufacturing industries, which became significant contributors to the economy. Factories emerged as hubs of employment, fostering urbanization and changes in the demographic landscape.

Urbanization gained momentum as rural populations moved to urban centers in search of employment and improved living conditions. Cities like Montevideo experienced a surge in population, leading to the expansion of urban spaces and changes in housing, infrastructure, and public services.

Social policies played a significant role in shaping the era. The introduction of social security, universal healthcare, and education reforms marked a commitment to social welfare and equity. These policies aimed to provide citizens with access to basic services and opportunities for upward mobility.

The nation's commitment to education extended beyond the classroom. Adult education programs, cultural institutions, and public libraries contributed to a culture of learning and intellectual enrichment. This emphasis on education and access to knowledge further shaped Uruguay's societal fabric.

Economic growth brought about changes in consumer patterns and lifestyles. The emergence of a middle class signaled increased purchasing power and a demand for consumer goods. This shift had implications for cultural norms, preferences, and the emergence of new forms of leisure and entertainment.

The mid-20th century also witnessed shifts in political dynamics. The presidency of Luis Batlle Berres brought about a period of political stability, characterized by policies that promoted social welfare, workers' rights, and urban development. Batlle Berres' legacy as a reformist leader resonates with Uruguay's ongoing commitment to social progress.

The era was not without its challenges. Economic fluctuations, inflation, and shifts in global trade patterns influenced Uruguay's economic stability. These challenges underscored the complexities of maintaining a balance between economic growth and social equity.

Cultural expressions also reflected the changing times. Literature, art, and music responded to the evolving societal dynamics, reflecting themes of urbanization, social change, and the challenges of modernity. Uruguayan cultural creators engaged with global artistic trends while infusing their works with a distinct national identity.

The era's legacy remains embedded in Uruguay's social and economic fabric. The policies, urban transformations, and societal shifts laid the groundwork for modern Uruguay, with many of the values and structures established during this time continuing to shape the nation's identity and progress.

The mid-20th century stands as a testament to Uruguay's ability to adapt to change, to navigate challenges, and to embrace policies and developments that prioritize social welfare and progress. As we explore this chapter, we uncover the layers of transformation, social policies, and economic shifts that have left an indelible mark on Uruguay's societal and economic landscape.

Under Dictatorship's Shadow: Challenging Years of Military Rule

The late 20th century bore witness to a tumultuous period in Uruguay's history, characterized by a series of military dictatorships that cast a shadow over the nation's political landscape. This chapter delves into the intricate tapestry of Uruguay's experience under military rule, exploring the rise of authoritarian regimes, human rights violations, resistance movements, and the lasting impact on the nation's democratic journey.

The first military dictatorship emerged in 1973 following a coup d'état that overthrew the civilian government. The armed forces, led by Juan María Bordaberry, seized power and embarked on a period of authoritarian rule. The coup marked a rupture in Uruguay's democratic tradition and set the stage for a challenging era.

The military regimes that followed implemented policies aimed at suppressing political dissent and curtailing civil liberties. Censorship of the press, limitations on freedom of expression, and arbitrary detentions became hallmarks of this period. The nation found itself grappling with a climate of fear and repression.

The policies of military rule were often justified under the pretext of combating left-wing guerrilla movements. The Tupamaros, a leftist urban guerrilla group, had gained notoriety for its activities in the 1960s. While these groups posed a challenge to the government, the military response extended beyond targeting militants to include broader segments of society.

Human rights violations during this era were widespread and deeply troubling. Reports of torture, forced disappearances, and extrajudicial killings highlighted the brutality of the regime. Many individuals were subject to persecution based on their political beliefs, and families were torn apart by the uncertainty of the fate of their loved ones.

The era also witnessed the emergence of a courageous resistance movement. Civil society, including labor unions, students, and human rights organizations, rallied against the repressive regime. These movements represented a beacon of hope in a time of darkness, demonstrating the resilience of the human spirit in the face of adversity.

International condemnation of the human rights abuses in Uruguay added pressure on the military regimes. The nation's tarnished image on the global stage prompted calls for change and justice. The persistence of human rights advocates and the determination of the international community played a role in shaping the eventual transition to democracy.

The gradual process of democratization began in the early 1980s. The nation's yearning for freedom, combined with international pressure, compelled the military regime to initiate steps towards restoring democratic governance. Negotiations between the regime and civilian political actors paved the way for democratic elections and a return to civilian rule.

The legacy of Uruguay's experience under military dictatorship remains a somber reminder of the fragility of democracy and the importance of safeguarding human rights. The courage of those who resisted and the commitment of those who sought justice have left a profound impact on Uruguay's contemporary democratic institutions and societal values.

Struggle for Human Rights: Resilience and Return to Democracy

The late 20th century witnessed a remarkable chapter in Uruguay's history as the nation emerged from the shadows of military dictatorship and embarked on a journey toward reclaiming its democratic values and human rights. This chapter delves into the intricate tapestry of Uruguay's struggle for human rights, the resilience of its people, and the path that led to the restoration of democratic governance.

The aftermath of military rule left Uruguay grappling with the legacies of human rights abuses, forced disappearances, and a fractured society. Families and communities were scarred by the loss of loved ones and the trauma of the past. The quest for truth, justice, and accountability became integral to the nation's healing process.

The tireless efforts of human rights organizations, activists, and families of victims played a pivotal role in bringing attention to the atrocities committed during the dictatorship. The Mothers and Relatives of Detained and Disappeared People, known as Madres y Familiares de Uruguayos Detenidos y Desaparecidos, became a symbol of resilience and a driving force in the pursuit of justice.

The testimonies of survivors and victims' families shone a light on the dark period of dictatorship, forcing the nation to confront its painful history. These narratives highlighted the urgency of acknowledging past wrongs and holding those responsible for human rights violations accountable.

The return to democracy was marked by a series of pivotal moments. The constitutional referendum of 1980, despite its flaws, reflected the nation's desire for a democratic transition. The negotiations between the military regime and civilian political actors paved the way for democratic elections and a restoration of civilian rule.

The 1984 presidential elections marked a watershed moment, as Uruguayans cast their votes in a free and fair electoral process. The election of Julio María Sanguinetti signaled the nation's commitment to democracy and a collective aspiration for a brighter future.

The transition to democracy was not without its challenges. The nation had to grapple with the complexities of addressing human rights violations while fostering national reconciliation. Efforts were made to establish truth commissions and judicial processes to investigate the crimes committed during the dictatorship.

The perseverance of civil society and human rights organizations contributed to the eventual accountability of those responsible for human rights abuses. Trials, investigations, and the pursuit of justice sent a powerful message that impunity would not prevail and that Uruguay was committed to upholding human rights norms.

The democratic era brought about institutional changes aimed at safeguarding human rights. Constitutional reforms, legal protections, and the establishment of institutions dedicated to human rights advocacy marked the nation's determination to ensure that the horrors of the past would not be repeated.

The resilience of Uruguayans in the face of adversity and their commitment to democracy and human rights became integral to the nation's identity. The struggle for human rights and the restoration of democratic governance stands as a testament to Uruguay's capacity to overcome challenges and to reassert its commitment to justice and freedom.

Montevideo: A Historical Portrait of Uruguay's Capital

Nestled along the eastern shore of the Rio de la Plata, Montevideo stands as the vibrant and historical heart of Uruguay. As the nation's capital, this city has witnessed centuries of transformation, from its humble beginnings as a Spanish settlement to its role as a modern and bustling metropolis. This chapter delves into the intricate tapestry of Montevideo's history, exploring its colonial roots, cultural evolution, architectural heritage, and the enduring spirit that defines the city.

Montevideo's history dates back to its establishment by the Spanish in 1724. Named after its geographic location, the city's name roughly translates to "I see the mountain" in Spanish, a nod to Cerro de Montevideo, a nearby hill that offers panoramic views of the city and the river.

The city's strategic location on the Rio de la Plata made it a key port for trade and maritime activities. Montevideo's natural harbor facilitated commerce, contributing to its growth as a commercial hub in the region. Over the centuries, the city's fortunes were shaped by its role as a port city and its interactions with global trade networks.

Montevideo's colonial architecture, characterized by cobbled streets, plazas, and historic buildings, reflects its Spanish heritage. The Ciudad Vieja, or Old Town, is a living testament to the city's history, with its colonial-era architecture juxtaposed against modern developments. The Matriz Square, featuring the Montevideo Metropolitan

Cathedral, stands as a historic center of religious and cultural significance.

The 19th century brought about a period of change and upheaval for Montevideo. The city played a central role in Uruguay's struggle for independence from Spanish colonial rule. It was the site of key battles and political negotiations that eventually led to the nation's autonomy.

Montevideo's cosmopolitan character began to take shape in the late 19th and early 20th centuries. Waves of immigrants, including Europeans and Middle Easterners, contributed to the city's cultural diversity. This diversity is evident in the city's architecture, neighborhoods, and culinary traditions.

The arts have flourished in Montevideo, with the city serving as a cultural hub for literature, music, and theater. The Teatro Solís, a historic theater dating back to the 19th century, stands as a symbol of the city's cultural heritage. The theater has hosted performances by renowned artists and continues to be a focal point of artistic expression.

Montevideo's coastline, stretching along the Rambla, offers breathtaking views of the Rio de la Plata. This picturesque waterfront promenade is a gathering place for residents and visitors alike, offering spaces for relaxation, recreation, and social interactions.

Modern Montevideo is a dynamic and bustling city that blends its historical past with contemporary developments. The city's financial district, Pocitos neighborhood, and cultural institutions contribute to its status as a dynamic metropolis. Montevideo's commitment to sustainability and green spaces is evident in its numerous parks and eco-friendly initiatives.

Montevideo's enduring spirit and cultural vibrancy continue to define its identity. The city's history, architecture, cultural expressions, and welcoming atmosphere make it a destination that invites exploration and reflection on Uruguay's past, present, and future.

Colonia del Sacramento: Tracing the Footprints of Portuguese and Spanish Heritage

Nestled along the banks of the Rio de la Plata, Colonia del Sacramento is a charming city that bears the indelible marks of both Portuguese and Spanish heritage. Its history is a tapestry woven from the threads of colonial conquest, strategic rivalry, and cultural exchange. This chapter delves into the intricate story of Colonia del Sacramento, exploring its origins, architectural legacy, and the unique blend of influences that make it a UNESCO World Heritage site.

Colonia del Sacramento's history can be traced back to its founding by the Portuguese in 1680. The city was established as a strategic outpost to assert Portuguese presence in the region and to counter Spanish ambitions in the Rio de la Plata basin. Its location, at the confluence of Spanish and Portuguese territories, made it a focal point of geopolitical competition.

The Spanish quickly recognized the importance of Colonia del Sacramento and sought to claim it for themselves. The city changed hands multiple times over the course of its early history, passing between Portuguese and Spanish control. These shifts in power left an imprint on the city's architecture, culture, and identity.

The historic quarter of Colonia del Sacramento, known as the Barrio Histórico, showcases the city's architectural heritage. Cobblestone streets wind through a collection of well-preserved colonial buildings, each telling a story of its own. The influence of both Portuguese and Spanish architecture is evident in the design of houses, churches, and fortifications.

One of the city's most iconic landmarks is the Plaza Mayor, a central square surrounded by colonial-era buildings. The Basílica del Santísimo Sacramento, a 17th-century church, stands as a testament to the city's religious history. Nearby, the ruins of the Convento de San Francisco offer a glimpse into the past and a reminder of the city's turbulent history.

The city's fortifications, including the Fortaleza del Colonia, reflect the strategic importance of Colonia del Sacramento in regional conflicts. These fortifications, designed to defend against potential invasions, provide insights into the military strategies and engineering prowess of the time.

Colonia del Sacramento's status as a UNESCO World Heritage site speaks to its cultural significance and historical value. The city's unique blend of Portuguese and Spanish influences has been carefully preserved, allowing visitors to step back in time and experience the echoes of its colonial past.

Cultural exchange between the two colonial powers is evident in Colonia's cuisine, language, and traditions. The city's culinary offerings reflect a fusion of Spanish and Portuguese flavors, while its local dialect features linguistic elements from both colonial legacies.

The city's rich history and architectural heritage have made it a popular destination for tourists seeking to immerse themselves in Uruguay's past. Colonia del Sacramento offers a serene escape from the bustle of modern life, allowing visitors to wander through its narrow streets, explore its museums, and appreciate the layers of history that have shaped its character.

Artigas: Tribute to the National Hero and His Legacy

José Gervasio Artigas, a towering figure in Uruguayan history, is revered as a national hero and a symbol of Uruguay's struggle for independence and social justice. This chapter pays homage to the life, contributions, and enduring legacy of Artigas, exploring his leadership, ideals, and the indelible mark he left on Uruguay's identity.

Born in 1764 in Montevideo, Artigas grew up in a region marked by colonial rivalries and social inequalities. His early experiences shaped his commitment to justice and his determination to challenge the status quo. As a young man, he witnessed the struggles of rural workers and indigenous communities, which ignited his passion for social reform.

Artigas's leadership emerged during the tumultuous times of the Spanish colonial period. He played a pivotal role in the fight against Spanish rule, organizing armed forces and leading a series of military campaigns. His vision extended beyond mere independence, encompassing the ideals of democracy, federalism, and equal rights for all citizens.

One of Artigas's most notable achievements was the establishment of the Liga Federal, a confederation of provinces that united against Spanish royalists and sought to promote regional autonomy and social justice. His leadership within the Liga Federal earned him the title of "Protector of the Free Peoples."

Artigas's influence extended beyond the battlefield. His writings and speeches articulated his vision for a just and inclusive society. He championed the rights of indigenous communities, workers, and peasants, advocating for land reform and social equality.

The legacy of Artigas was not confined to his military and political endeavors. His role as a unifying figure became evident during the Siege of Montevideo, a critical battle for Uruguay's independence. Artigas's leadership and ability to unite diverse factions played a crucial role in securing victory.

Despite his efforts, Artigas's vision for a federal, egalitarian nation faced challenges. Internal divisions within the Liga Federal, as well as external pressures from neighboring powers, led to his eventual exile. Artigas spent his later years in Paraguay, where he continued to advocate for his ideals.

Artigas's legacy reverberates through Uruguay's cultural fabric. His memory is honored through monuments, statues, and institutions dedicated to preserving his contributions. The Artigas Mausoleum, located in the Plaza Independencia in Montevideo, serves as a symbolic resting place for his remains and a reminder of his enduring significance.

Artigas's influence is not limited to Uruguay; it extends to the broader region. His ideals of federalism, social justice, and sovereignty influenced other Latin American leaders and movements. His legacy lives on in the struggles for democracy, human rights, and social equality.

In contemporary Uruguay, Artigas remains a touchstone of national identity and values. His legacy continues to inspire civic engagement, social justice activism, and a commitment to democratic ideals. Artigas's embodiment of courage, resilience, and unwavering principles stands as a testament to the power of individual leadership in shaping a nation's destiny.

Rivera: Uruguay's Borderland and Cultural Confluence

Nestled along Uruguay's northern border with Brazil, Rivera is a region that epitomizes the nation's geographical diversity and cultural interplay. This chapter delves into the intricate tapestry of Rivera, exploring its unique position as a borderland, its cultural blend, historical significance, and the ways in which it reflects the complexities of Uruguay's identity.

Rivera's location on the border with Brazil has endowed it with a distinct character. It serves as a gateway between two nations, each with its own history, language, and cultural traditions. This geographical proximity has contributed to the region's role as a cultural confluence, where Uruguayan and Brazilian influences converge.

The region's history is intertwined with cross-border dynamics. The city of Rivera itself was named after General Fructuoso Rivera, a key figure in Uruguay's fight for independence. The region has witnessed historical events, trade interactions, and cultural exchanges that have left an indelible mark on its identity.

One of the most iconic features of Rivera is the International Bridge of the Free Peoples, which connects the city to the Brazilian town of Santana do Livramento. This bridge symbolizes the spirit of cooperation between Uruguay and Brazil, facilitating trade, tourism, and social interactions. The confluence of cultures in Rivera is palpable in various aspects of daily life. The region's gastronomy, for instance, reflects a fusion of Uruguayan and Brazilian flavors. Local dishes incorporate ingredients and culinary techniques from both sides of the border, resulting in a unique culinary experience.

The linguistic landscape of Rivera is equally fascinating. Due to its proximity to Brazil, Portuguese is commonly spoken alongside Spanish. This linguistic diversity adds to the region's rich cultural tapestry and underscores its role as a crossroads of languages and identities. Rivera's economy is closely tied to its borderland status. The city has evolved into a commercial hub, attracting shoppers from both Uruguay and Brazil. The city's markets and shopping centers bustle with activity as visitors seek a diverse array of products from both sides of the border.

The cultural exchanges that occur in Rivera extend beyond commerce. Festivals, events, and celebrations provide opportunities for people from both nations to come together and celebrate their shared heritage. These gatherings offer a glimpse into the cultural ties that bind the region.

The rich history of Rivera is also evident in its architecture and landmarks. Historical sites, plazas, and museums offer insights into the region's past and its role in Uruguay's history. These sites pay homage to the cultural interplay that has shaped Rivera's identity.

Rivera's role as a borderland and cultural confluence extends beyond physical boundaries. It symbolizes the interconnectedness of nations, the resilience of cultural identities, and the power of collaboration. The region's history, languages, cuisines, and traditions stand as a testament to the strength of diversity and the ways in which it enriches society.

Treasures of Biodiversity: Exploring Uruguay's Wildlife

Uruguay's natural landscapes are a treasure trove of biodiversity, offering a diverse array of ecosystems and habitats that support a rich variety of wildlife. From lush wetlands to expansive grasslands, this chapter delves into the intricate tapestry of Uruguay's wildlife, exploring its unique flora and fauna, conservation efforts, and the importance of preserving these natural wonders for future generations.

The wetlands of Uruguay, notably the Esteros de Farrapos e Islas del Río Uruguay, are a haven for birdlife. These wetlands provide crucial nesting and feeding grounds for over 300 bird species, including herons, ibises, and waterfowl. The Laguna de Rocha, designated a National Park, is another hotspot for birdwatching enthusiasts, where migratory species gather during their journeys.

The grasslands, or pampas, that stretch across Uruguay's interior are home to a variety of wildlife species. Among them is the capybara, the world's largest rodent, which can be spotted in wetland areas. The maned wolf, a unique and elusive carnivore, roams the grasslands in search of prey.

The Atlantic coastline of Uruguay supports a diverse marine ecosystem. La Coronilla, a coastal town, is home to one of the largest sea lion colonies in the region. These marine mammals can be observed basking on the beaches and rocks, offering a glimpse into the underwater world of Uruguay.

The Atlantic Forest, which extends into Uruguay's northeastern region, is recognized as one of the world's biodiversity hotspots. This lush forest is inhabited by a variety of species, including the rare and elusive jaguar. Conservation efforts in this region aim to protect both the habitat and the species that call it home.

Uruguay's commitment to wildlife conservation is evident through its network of protected areas and national parks. The Cabo Polonio National Park, for instance, safeguards a unique coastal ecosystem where visitors can spot native flora and fauna, including the tuco-tuco, a small burrowing rodent.

The efforts to protect Uruguay's wildlife extend beyond national borders. The country is a signatory to international conservation agreements and works collaboratively to preserve migratory bird routes and marine ecosystems. These partnerships reflect Uruguay's dedication to global biodiversity conservation.

Education and ecotourism play a pivotal role in raising awareness about the importance of preserving Uruguay's wildlife. Eco-lodges, guided tours, and educational programs offer opportunities for visitors to experience the country's natural wonders while fostering an understanding of the need for conservation.

Challenges such as habitat loss, pollution, and climate change pose threats to Uruguay's wildlife. Efforts to address these challenges include reforestation projects, sustainable land management practices, and research initiatives to better understand the needs of different species.

The diversity of Uruguay's wildlife showcases the intricate interplay between ecosystems and the species that inhabit them. From the smallest insects to the largest mammals, each contributes to the delicate balance that sustains life in Uruguay's natural landscapes.

Culinary Kaleidoscope: Uruguayan Cuisine Through the Ages

Uruguayan cuisine is a reflection of the nation's history, culture, and the diverse influences that have shaped its culinary landscape over the centuries. From indigenous ingredients to European flavors, this chapter delves into the intricate tapestry of Uruguayan cuisine, exploring its evolution, signature dishes, and the ways in which it captures the essence of the country.

Uruguay's indigenous peoples, including the Charrúa and Guarani, played a fundamental role in shaping the culinary foundation of the nation. Ingredients like maize, beans, squash, and potatoes formed the basis of their diet. These ingredients continue to influence modern Uruguayan cuisine, finding their way into traditional dishes.

The arrival of Spanish colonizers in the 16th century introduced new ingredients and culinary techniques. European flavors began to merge with indigenous traditions, giving rise to a unique fusion of flavors. The asado, a quintessential Uruguayan barbecue, is a prime example of this blending, with Spanish grilling methods meeting local meats.

The asado, characterized by the slow grilling of various cuts of meat over an open flame, is more than just a meal—it's a cultural tradition. The ritual of gathering around the grill, known as the parrilla, is a cornerstone of Uruguayan social life. The asado brings together family and friends to enjoy the flavors and camaraderie that define Uruguay's culinary culture.

Uruguay's European influences expanded beyond Spain to include Italian and Basque immigrants. These immigrants brought with them their own culinary traditions, which enriched the nation's gastronomic tapestry. Italian-style pasta dishes, particularly gnocchi, became a beloved part of Uruguay's culinary landscape.

Uruguay's coastal location also plays a pivotal role in its cuisine. Seafood, including fish and shellfish, features prominently in dishes along the Atlantic coastline. The coastal town of Punta del Este, for instance, is known for its fresh seafood offerings that draw both locals and visitors alike.

Mate, a traditional South American infused drink made from the leaves of the yerba mate plant, is a staple of Uruguayan culture. Sharing mate is a social practice that fosters connections and conversations. The ritual of preparing and sharing mate is deeply ingrained in the daily lives of Uruguayans.

Uruguayan sweets and desserts are a reflection of the nation's multicultural influences. Postres like chajá, a meringue and fruit dessert, showcase a blend of European and local ingredients. Dulce de leche, a sweet milk caramel, is an integral component of many Uruguayan desserts, adding a rich and indulgent flavor.

Modern Uruguayan cuisine continues to evolve, embracing global trends while remaining rooted in tradition. Chefs and culinary enthusiasts experiment with fusion cuisine, infusing traditional dishes with contemporary twists. Farmto-table initiatives highlight the importance of locally sourced ingredients and sustainability.

The culinary kaleidoscope of Uruguay captures the nation's spirit, history, and diversity. Whether savoring a succulent asado, sharing mate with friends, or indulging in a sweet dulce de leche treat, the flavors of Uruguay evoke a sense of belonging and community. Uruguayan cuisine is a reflection of a nation that celebrates its past while looking forward to a flavorful future.

Echoes of the Past: UNESCO World Heritage Sites in Uruguay

Uruguay is home to a collection of UNESCO World Heritage Sites that embody the nation's rich history, cultural significance, and architectural legacy. These sites serve as windows into Uruguay's past, offering glimpses into the diverse influences that have shaped the country's identity over the centuries. This chapter delves into the captivating stories behind Uruguay's UNESCO World Heritage Sites, exploring their historical contexts, architectural marvels, and the efforts to preserve these treasures for future generations.

1. Colonia del Sacramento: The historic quarter of Colonia del Sacramento, with its cobblestone streets and colonial architecture, was inscribed as a UNESCO World Heritage Site in 1995. Its history dates back to the 17th century, with Portuguese and Spanish influences interwoven into its streets, plazas, and buildings. The site's architecture reflects its strategic importance as a border town and a hub of trade.

2. Fray Bentos Industrial Landscape: This site, added to the list in 2015, showcases the remnants of the Liebig's Extract of Meat Company's industrial complex. Located in Fray Bentos, this complex played a significant role in the meatpacking industry during the late 19th and early 20th centuries. The site stands as a testament to Uruguay's industrial past and its contribution to global food production.

3. Quebrada de los Cuervos: Designated as a UNESCO World Heritage Site in 2016, Quebrada de los Cuervos is a natural wonder that boasts unique geological formations and lush landscapes. This protected area is home to diverse plant and animal species, making it a haven for ecotourism and outdoor enthusiasts.

4. Historic Quarter of the City of Santa Teresa and Fortress of Santa Teresa: This site, inscribed in 2016, encapsulates Uruguay's military history and architectural heritage. The fortress, built during the colonial period, stands as a symbol of Uruguay's strategic importance and its role in regional conflicts.

5. San Miguel Agricultural Colony: Added to the list in 2015, this site represents the efforts of Swiss settlers to establish an agricultural colony in the late 19th century. The colony's layout, architecture, and farming practices reflect the resilience and determination of these immigrants.

6. Artigas Mausoleum: Located in the Plaza Independencia in Montevideo, this mausoleum is dedicated to José Gervasio Artigas, Uruguay's national hero. His legacy and ideals are honored through this monument, which became a UNESCO World Heritage Site in 2010.

These UNESCO World Heritage Sites in Uruguay showcase the nation's commitment to preserving its cultural and natural heritage. The designation not only highlights the importance of these sites within Uruguay's narrative but also places them on the global stage as places of historical and cultural significance.

Efforts to conserve and safeguard these sites are ongoing, with preservation initiatives, restoration projects, and educational programs in place. These efforts ensure that these sites remain accessible for generations to come, allowing visitors and residents alike to connect with Uruguay's past, understand its cultural richness, and appreciate the architectural marvels that dot the nation's landscape.

Punta del Este: The Glamour and Natural Beauty of Uruguay's Beaches

Punta del Este, often referred to as the "St. Tropez of South America," is a coastal gem that has captivated visitors with its luxurious ambiance, stunning beaches, and vibrant cultural scene. This chapter dives into the allure of Punta del Este, exploring its evolution from a sleepy fishing village to a glamorous international destination known for its pristine beaches, upscale resorts, and a unique blend of natural beauty and cosmopolitan flair.

Nestled on a peninsula that juts into the Atlantic Ocean, Punta del Este boasts a breathtaking coastline that stretches for miles. Its beaches, with their golden sands and crystal-clear waters, have become synonymous with relaxation, recreation, and the quintessential beach getaway. Playa Brava, facing the open ocean, is known for its iconic sculpture of a hand emerging from the sand—a symbol of Punta del Este's artistic spirit and its connection to the sea.

Playa Mansa, on the opposite side of the peninsula, offers calm waters ideal for swimming, kayaking, and other water activities. This beach is a favorite among families and those seeking a tranquil seaside experience. The sunset views over the bay create a picturesque backdrop for romantic strolls along the shore.

Punta del Este's allure is not limited to its natural beauty; it's also a playground for the rich and famous. The city's luxury resorts, upscale boutiques, and high-end restaurants cater to an elite clientele seeking refined experiences and top-notch amenities. Visitors can indulge in spa treatments, enjoy gourmet dining, and experience the epitome of comfort and elegance. The city's vibrant cultural scene sets it apart from other beach destinations. Punta del Este hosts an array of art galleries, cultural centers, and annual events that celebrate art, music, and theater. The International Film Festival of Punta del Este and the Biennial of Contemporary Art are examples of the city's commitment to fostering creativity and cultural exchange.

Punta del Este's nightlife is equally dynamic, with a variety of bars, clubs, and entertainment venues that come alive after the sun sets. The city's casino, renowned for its elegance and sophistication, adds a touch of glamour to the evening scene.

Beyond the city's bustling center lies the serene natural beauty of the surrounding landscapes. The nearby Isla de Lobos is home to the largest sea lion colony in the Southern Hemisphere. Boat tours offer visitors a chance to witness these majestic marine mammals in their natural habitat.

Ecotourism opportunities abound as well, with nearby wetlands, dunes, and nature reserves inviting exploration. Laguna del Sauce, a freshwater lake, offers water-based activities such as kayaking and sailing, allowing visitors to connect with Uruguay's natural beauty beyond its beaches.

Punta del Este's blend of natural allure, cultural vibrancy, and upscale offerings has made it a sought-after destination for travelers from around the world. The city's ability to harmonize its luxurious amenities with its coastal charm speaks to its unique character—a place where glamour and natural beauty coexist in harmony.

Tacuarembó: Cradle of Folklore and Rich Musical Traditions

Nestled in the heart of Uruguay, Tacuarembó stands as a cultural epicenter, celebrated for its rich musical traditions, vibrant folkloric heritage, and its profound impact on Uruguay's artistic landscape. This chapter delves into the cultural tapestry of Tacuarembó, exploring its historical significance, its pivotal role in preserving and promoting folk music, and the ways in which it has contributed to shaping the nation's musical identity.

Tacuarembó's influence on Uruguay's musical heritage is deeply rooted in its history and geography. The city's central location allowed it to become a crossroads for various cultural influences, blending indigenous rhythms, European melodies, and African beats. This fusion of musical elements created a unique sonic palette that would later define the region's folkloric traditions.

One of the most iconic figures to emerge from Tacuarembó is Carlos Gardel, known as the "King of Tango." Although born in France, Gardel spent his early years in Tacuarembó, and his music reflects the cultural diversity of the region. His tango compositions continue to resonate globally, and his legacy has solidified Tacuarembó's reputation as a breeding ground for musical talent.

Tacuarembó's contribution to folk music is exemplified by the Festival Nacional del Folclore, an annual event that gathers musicians, dancers, and enthusiasts from all corners of Uruguay. This festival, inaugurated in 1958, celebrates traditional music, dance, and customs, providing a platform for emerging and established artists to showcase their talents.

The region's musical heritage extends beyond tango and folk music. Tacuarembó is also renowned for its payadores, improvisational poets and musicians who engage in poetic duels, blending humor, wit, and musicality. Payadores have played a pivotal role in preserving oral traditions and storytelling, passing down tales from one generation to the next.

In addition to its musical contributions, Tacuarembó is home to the Museo Carlos Gardel, a museum dedicated to the life and legacy of the tango icon. The museum offers visitors a glimpse into Gardel's early years, his artistic journey, and the impact he had on shaping the tango genre.

Tacuarembó's commitment to its musical traditions is evident in its efforts to provide education and training to aspiring musicians. Music schools, workshops, and cultural centers offer opportunities for individuals to develop their talents, ensuring the continuity of the region's musical legacy.

The region's love for music is not confined to formal settings. Street festivals, neighborhood gatherings, and spontaneous jam sessions are common occurrences in Tacuarembó, highlighting the organic and communal nature of its musical culture.

Lavalleja: Remembering the Great Battle and Embracing Nature

Lavalleja, a region steeped in history and natural beauty, holds a special place in Uruguay's narrative. This chapter delves into Lavalleja's historical significance, particularly its association with the Great Battle of 1836, and its deep connection to the natural landscapes that have shaped its identity as a haven for outdoor enthusiasts and history buffs alike.

Lavalleja's most defining moment in history was the Great Battle of 1836, also known as the Battle of Carpintería. This pivotal clash between the Blanco and Colorado political factions marked a turning point in Uruguay's struggle for independence. Led by Juan Antonio Lavalleja, the Colorado forces emerged victorious, paving the way for Uruguay's autonomy and the establishment of its identity as an independent nation.

The legacy of the Great Battle is preserved in Lavalleja through monuments, memorials, and museums that pay homage to the sacrifices made and the ideals fought for. The Museo Histórico Nacional de la Batalla de Las Piedras in the town of Las Piedras offers visitors an opportunity to delve into the history of the battle and gain insights into the socio-political context of the time.

Lavalleja's natural landscapes are equally captivating. The region is part of the Cerro Largo department, characterized by rolling hills, fertile valleys, and lush grasslands. It is a paradise for hikers, nature lovers, and those seeking solace in the embrace of unspoiled wilderness.

Quebrada de los Cuervos, a natural reserve located in Lavalleja, is a testament to the region's natural wonders. This stunning gorge is adorned with waterfalls, lush vegetation, and unique geological formations. Visitors can embark on hiking trails that offer panoramic views and a chance to connect with nature on a profound level.

Lavalleja's commitment to conservation is evident in the establishment of protected areas and natural reserves. The Sierra de las Ánimas Natural Park, for instance, safeguards a diverse range of ecosystems, from grasslands to forests. This dedication to preserving the region's biodiversity ensures that future generations can enjoy its natural beauty.

The town of Minas, the departmental capital of Lavalleja, serves as a hub for both history and outdoor exploration. Its colonial architecture, charming plazas, and historical landmarks evoke a sense of nostalgia for Uruguay's past. Nearby attractions like the Salto del Penitente, a picturesque waterfall, offer opportunities for adventure and relaxation.

The Lavalleja department's sense of community is deeply rooted in its history and natural surroundings. Festivals, cultural events, and celebrations bring residents and visitors together to honor their heritage, appreciate their landscapes, and forge connections that reflect the region's warm hospitality.

Paysandú: From Historic Siege to Cultural Abundance

Paysandú, a city that has witnessed pivotal moments in Uruguay's history, stands as a testament to resilience, cultural diversity, and the enduring spirit of its people. This chapter delves into Paysandú's past, marked by the historic Siege of Paysandú, and explores how the city has evolved into a cultural hub that celebrates its heritage and offers a wealth of artistic and recreational opportunities.

One of the most significant events in Paysandú's history is the Siege of Paysandú, which unfolded in 1864 during the larger context of the War of the Triple Alliance. The city's defenders valiantly resisted the siege by Paraguayan forces, and the intense battle left a lasting mark on Paysandú's collective memory. The city's motto "Heroica" pays tribute to the bravery displayed during this challenging period.

The legacy of the siege is kept alive through memorials, monuments, and historical sites. The Plaza Constitución, Paysandú's central square, is home to a monument dedicated to the defenders of the city. This site serves as a poignant reminder of the sacrifices made to protect Paysandú's sovereignty.

Paysandú's cultural scene is a vibrant reflection of its diverse heritage. The city's Teatro Florencio Sánchez, inaugurated in 1876, is one of the oldest theaters in Uruguay and hosts a variety of theatrical productions, concerts, and cultural events. The theater is named after Florencio Sánchez, a renowned Uruguayan playwright, highlighting Paysandú's contribution to the nation's literary and artistic legacy.

The city's commitment to the arts extends to its Museo Histórico Departamental, a museum that preserves and showcases Paysandú's history through artifacts, documents, and exhibitions. The museum provides insights into the region's development, cultural exchanges, and the impact of significant events such as the siege.

Paysandú's natural beauty is also a point of pride. The city is situated along the Uruguay River, offering picturesque views and recreational opportunities along its banks. The Parque Municipal is a serene green space that invites residents and visitors to unwind, enjoy outdoor activities, and connect with nature.

Paysandú's role as a cultural center is exemplified by its annual Carnival celebration, which attracts participants and spectators from across Uruguay and beyond. The city comes alive with colorful parades, music, dance, and artistic displays, showcasing the diversity and vibrancy of Uruguayan culture.

The gastronomic scene in Paysandú is another dimension of its cultural abundance. Local restaurants and eateries offer a variety of dishes that celebrate regional flavors and culinary traditions. Uruguay's national dish, the asado, is a staple at many local establishments, allowing visitors to savor the country's famed barbecue culture.

Durazno: Tracing Agricultural Heritage and Heartland Traditions

Nestled in the heart of Uruguay, Durazno stands as a testament to the nation's agricultural heritage and the enduring traditions that have shaped its identity. This chapter delves into the rich history of Durazno, exploring its agricultural significance, the pivotal role it plays in Uruguay's economy, and the authentic heartland traditions that define its culture.

Durazno's roots are deeply intertwined with agriculture, earning it the moniker "Fruit Basket of Uruguay." The city's name itself, "Durazno," translates to "peach," a nod to the abundant fruit orchards that once adorned its landscape. The fertile soils and favorable climate of the region have made it a prime location for agricultural activities, ranging from fruit cultivation to livestock farming.

Agriculture has been the cornerstone of Durazno's economy for generations. The region's fields yield a diverse range of crops, including citrus fruits, grapes, soybeans, and wheat. These crops contribute significantly to Uruguay's agricultural exports and play a vital role in ensuring food security for the nation and beyond.

The Estadio Ingeniero Raúl Saturnino Goyenola, Durazno's multi-purpose stadium, serves as a symbol of the city's sporting and cultural legacy. It hosts a variety of events, including soccer matches and cultural festivals, providing a space for both recreation and community gatherings.

Durazno's heartland traditions are celebrated through its annual folk festivals and events. The Fiesta Nacional de la Primavera, or National Spring Festival, is a vibrant celebration that marks the arrival of spring. The festival features colorful parades, live music performances, and a sense of camaraderie that reflects the city's strong sense of community.

The city's cultural heritage is preserved and celebrated through institutions like the Museo Departamental de Durazno, a museum that showcases artifacts, documents, and exhibitions that shed light on Durazno's history, culture, and agricultural heritage. The museum serves as a repository of the city's collective memory and offers visitors insights into its evolution over time.

Durazno's connection to its rural traditions is further exemplified by its annual Rural Expo. This event showcases the region's agricultural products, livestock, and equestrian skills. It provides a platform for farmers and agribusinesses to showcase their innovations and contribute to the continued growth of Uruguay's agricultural sector.

The city's picturesque surroundings are a testament to its natural beauty. The Río Yí, a meandering river that flows through Durazno, offers opportunities for boating, fishing, and relaxation along its banks. The verdant landscapes and open spaces invite residents and visitors alike to connect with nature and enjoy outdoor activities.

Rocha: Coastal Charms and Environmental Conservation Efforts

Rocha, a coastal gem of Uruguay, is a place of unparalleled natural beauty, where pristine beaches, diverse ecosystems, and a commitment to environmental conservation come together in harmony. This chapter delves into the allure of Rocha, exploring its breathtaking coastal charms, its dedication to preserving its ecological treasures, and the unique blend of relaxation and adventure it offers to visitors.

Rocha's coastline is a tapestry of stunning beaches, each with its own distinctive character. Playa de la Paloma, with its golden sands and turquoise waters, is a popular spot for sunbathing, swimming, and water sports. Playa La Aguada, known for its strong waves, attracts surfers seeking the perfect wave and a thrilling ride.

Punta del Diablo, a fishing village turned bohemian beach town, exudes a laid-back vibe that captivates travelers. Its pristine beaches and bohemian atmosphere make it a haven for those seeking tranquility and a connection to nature. Nearby, Santa Teresa National Park offers a range of activities, from hiking through lush forests to exploring ancient fortifications.

Rocha's commitment to environmental conservation is reflected in its protected areas and initiatives. The Cabo Polonio National Park, a remote and off-the-grid destination, is a shining example of sustainable tourism. Its unique landscapes and abundant wildlife are preserved, and visitors are encouraged to appreciate the beauty of nature while minimizing their impact on the environment.

The Laguna de Rocha, a coastal lagoon teeming with biodiversity, has been designated a UNESCO Biosphere Reserve. This recognition underscores the importance of preserving the delicate balance of ecosystems in the area and promoting sustainable practices that protect both the land and sea.

Rocha's cultural scene is also a reflection of its coastal charms. The town of La Paloma hosts an annual International Film Festival, attracting cinephiles and creatives from around the world. The festival's focus on culture, art, and cinema aligns with Rocha's commitment to celebrating both its natural beauty and its creative spirit.

Local cuisine in Rocha is deeply rooted in its coastal setting. Seafood dishes, particularly fresh fish and succulent seafood platters, highlight the region's culinary offerings. These dishes allow visitors to savor the flavors of the sea while enjoying the picturesque coastal backdrop.

Rocha's proximity to nature invites exploration beyond the beaches. Cabo Polonio's shifting sand dunes and unique landscapes provide an otherworldly experience, while birdwatching in the Laguna de Rocha unveils a world of vibrant avian species.

Conclusion

The history of Uruguay is a tapestry woven from the threads of diverse cultures, significant events, and the indomitable spirit of its people. From its ancient indigenous civilizations to its struggles for independence, the formation of a nation, and the cultural blossoming of the modern era, Uruguay's journey has been marked by resilience, evolution, and a deep connection to its heritage.

Throughout this exploration, we've delved into Uruguay's rich past, tracing its geological origins, pre-colonial cultures, early encounters with European explorers, and the complex colonial period under Spanish rule. We witnessed the struggles for independence that culminated in Uruguay's emergence as a sovereign nation and followed its evolution through the 19th and 20th centuries, marked by political shifts, cultural advancements, and global participation.

From the agricultural heartlands of Durazno to the coastal charms of Rocha, the stories of individual cities and regions mirror the nation's multifaceted identity. We celebrated the agricultural heritage of Durazno, the heroic history of Paysandú, and the cultural renaissance of Montevideo. We marveled at the natural beauty of Rocha and explored the heartland traditions of Durazno.

In the midst of Uruguay's historical narrative, we discovered its dedication to conservation and environmental stewardship. The commitment to preserving the nation's ecological treasures, evident in places like Cabo Polonio and Laguna de Rocha, reflects Uruguay's recognition of the need to safeguard its natural beauty for future generations.

From the captivating rhythms of tango to the poetic verses of payadores, Uruguay's cultural legacy is a testament to its rich tapestry of traditions. The nation's role in global conflicts, its contributions to literature, music, and sports, and its embrace of democracy and human rights illustrate its journey toward progress and inclusivity.

As we close the chapter on this exploration, we're reminded that Uruguay's story is far from stagnant—it continues to unfold with each passing day. The history, culture, and traditions discussed in these pages form the foundation upon which Uruguay stands today, a nation that has weathered challenges, celebrated achievements, and embraced diversity. Through the lens of its history, we see a nation that values its past while embracing its present, with its eyes firmly set on the future. The history of Uruguay is not just a record of events; it's a living narrative that continues to shape the nation's identity, values, and aspirations for generations to come.

Thank you for embarking on this captivating journey through the history of Uruguay. We hope that the chapters within this book have provided you with a deeper understanding of the nation's past, its rich cultural heritage, and its enduring spirit. From the ancient indigenous civilizations to the modern-day cultural renaissance, Uruguay's story is a testament to resilience, evolution, and the power of heritage.

If you've enjoyed this exploration and found value in the insights shared, we kindly invite you to leave a positive review. Your feedback will not only help us improve our work but also encourage other readers to embark on this enlightening journey as well.

Once again, we express our gratitude for your time and interest. We hope that the pages of this book have left you with a sense of connection to Uruguay's history and a renewed appreciation for the tapestry of cultures that have shaped this remarkable nation.

Made in the USA
Las Vegas, NV
29 December 2023